Original title:
The Sun on Your Skin

Copyright © 2025 Creative Arts Management OÜ
All rights reserved.

Author: Milo Harrington
ISBN HARDBACK: 978-1-80581-695-9
ISBN PAPERBACK: 978-1-80581-222-7
ISBN EBOOK: 978-1-80581-695-9

Chasing Shadows in Golden Hours

In fields where giggles dance around,
We sprint like sprightly ants, unbound.
The shadows stretch, they mock our chase,
While golden rays paint every face.

With ice cream drips and sticky hands,
We map our adventures, not just plans.
The sun above seems to conspire,
As we create our own mad choir.

Heatbeats and Solstice Skies

Tickling toes in the warm, bright light,
Chasing dreams that take full flight.
A goofy hat on a head so bare,
We laugh at our silliness, without a care.

The days are long, the laughs are loud,
We dance like fools, so unbowed.
Sipping lemonade with chubby cheeks,
In the warmth, it's joy our heart seeks.

Solitude Wrapped in Warmth

A cozy nook beneath a tree,
Where thoughts can bounce and hearts fly free.
I talk to squirrels, they munch on snacks,
While sunlight glimmers on laid-back backs.

The world might rush, but here I dwell,
In gentle rays, I weave my spell.
With every whisper of the breeze,
I giggle with the buzzing bees.

Laughter in the Radiant Glow

We race the shadows as they play,
Our laughter echoing the cloudy gray.
With silly games and cloudy dreams,
Life is fun, or so it seems.

A bumpy ride on a wheeled contraption,
We bound through life with giddy action.
In this warm glow, we're carefree fools,
Spun by sunshine, no time for rules.

Colors Painted by the Daystar

A splash of yellow, oh so bright,
Like a golden cat, basking in light.
Red hedgehogs roll in joyful glee,
While blue birds dance like they're on tea.

Pavement sizzles, shoes feel bold,
Sweaty brows, stories unfold.
Flip-flops flop, they rule the street,
While sunburns tell tales of defeat.

Ice cream drips, laughter rings,
Chasing shadows like playful things.
Watermelons wink in the heat,
Summer's mischief can't be beat.

Dancing daisies in a line,
Glimpse of laughter, pure divine.
Colors mesh in wild parade,
Under playful rays, we're made.

When Warmth Meets the Skin

Skin feels tingly, what a treat,
It's like a bear hug from the heat.
Sunscreen battles, who will win?
A slippery mess—smiles begin!

Flip flops slap, the rhythm swings,
Silly hats with outrageous blings.
A picnic feast on grassy knoll,
But ants all crash our perfect stroll.

Birds dressed fancy fly and tease,
While bees zoom past with sweet expertise.
Sunbathers chat, and laughter soars,
In the warm embrace, we all explore.

Tan lines form, art in the making,
Bold fashion choices, is that baking?
With every ray, a funny tale,
As warmth strikes laughter without fail.

Soft Glow of Morning's Kiss

Early light peeks through the blinds,
Soft warmth tickles, like gentle winds.
Coffee brews, a rise and shine,
Work in pajamas? Oh, divine!

Socks unmatched, a fashion statement,
Toast pops up, quite the placement.
Sunbeams slide like sneaky thieves,
Through kitchen windows—could this be leaves?

A dance with shadows, toe to toe,
Cheerful giggles, twirls, and fro.
Eggs are scrambled, what a sight,
A sunny side up, oh what delight!

Morning's glow in silly ways,
Sets the mood for joyful plays.
Each new day, a chance to jest,
With warmth and laughter, we are blessed.

The Radiance of Life's Moments

Laughing children on the green,
Umbrellas fly, an unseen scene.
Silly games in joyful strides,
With cheers and giggles, pure sun tides.

Cotton candy clouds float high,
As growing we seem to defy.
Picnic baskets, crumbs abound,
While ants invade our merry ground.

Silly selfies in the rays,
Wacky poses brighten days.
Bouncing balls and sprightly runs,
Life's bright moments, filled with puns.

Chasing sunsets, shadows play,
In warm embrace, we stumble, sway.
With every twinkle, laughter beams,
As life's radiance fuels our dreams.

Awakening to the Softest Touch

A gentle nudge begins the day,
It tickles toes as we sway.
Pajamas cling, just a bit too tight,
Shadows stretch into the light.

The cat rolls over, seeking warmth,
His belly catches beams, a charm.
While I sip coffee, feeling bright,
Trying to wake up from the night.

The Embrace of Daylight's Lullaby

Morning whispers in my ear,
A symphony that's all too clear.
With breakfast eggs and squeaky chair,
The day arrives with utmost flair.

The toast pops up, and I yelp loud,
In golden glow, feeling proud.
With butter sliding down the side,
Who knew joy could be so wide?

Reflections of Warm Light

Mirrors gleam with a playful tease,
As I walk by, they laugh with ease.
My hair's a nest, my clothes a jumble,
Yet in the light, I dare to tumble.

The plants are glowing, swaying by,
In faux ballet, they dance and sigh.
I try to shine, but trip on a shoe,
Stumbling bright, as friendships do.

Golden Tides of Earth's Wonder

The world glimmers in a quirky way,
As I lose my hat in yesterday's play.
Breezes chase, and laughter rings,
Under the warmth, I feel such things.

The ice cream melts, I scramble quick,
A sticky delight—what a funny trick!
Laughter spreads as the colors swirl,
In golden waves, we jump and twirl.

Day's Gentle Touch on Reality

Waking up with sticky feet,
Coffee spills, oh what a treat!
Birds are chirping, can't you hear?
Life's a circus, give a cheer!

Sweat drops roll down my nose,
Chasing ice cream as it grows.
Why's my lemonade gone so fast?
Playing games, this fun won't last!

Flickers of Light Upon the Soul

A lantern made of skin and cheer,
Dancing shadows, lend an ear.
Sunbeams tickle, laughter flies,
Mom's old stories, full of lies!

Swimming pools and bright beach balls,
Splashes, giggles, summer calls.
Is that a tan or just sunburn?
In this warmth, the world can turn!

Emblazoned with Summer's Glow

My shirt's a canvas, dripped in tea,
Sticky fingers, wild and free.
Funny hats and pair of shades,
Trying hard to impress mermaids!

Mosquitoes buzzing, take a bite,
They find me tasty, what a fright!
In this glow, let's dance around,
With laughter, let our joy abound!

A Canvas Warmed by Solar Rays

Slathered in lotion, I take my stance,
Doing my best to pull off a dance.
Umbrella drinks with tiny straws,
Belly laughs, let's break some laws!

Sipping smoothies, flip-flops squeak,
Watch my sunscreen middle leak.
World's a stage, with sun-kissed dreams,
Join the laughter, or so it seems!

Vibrancy Wrapped in Warmth

Oh, how the rays do tickle me,
Like playful cats on a sunny spree.
With laughter loud, I twirl and spin,
In this bright warmth, let the fun begin.

Dancing shadows, a slapstick chase,
Who knew bright light could win this race?
As I chase my hat down the lane,
Oh, the silly joys that soothe my brain.

Caressing Day's Embrace

A glow that wraps like grandma's shawl,
Makes me trip and tumble—oh, I fall!
Blushing cheeks like ripe cherry pie,
Can't help but grin as the moments fly.

Mood swings swing like the branches high,
Chasing butterflies from ground to sky.
Watch me slip on a sunlit grin,
Hey, look at me, I'm back again!

Joy from Above, Love Within

Wink from the clouds, a cheeky tease,
Warmth drapes over with such sweet ease.
Dancing ants cause a silly fuss,
While I contemplate life from my bus.

Oh, my ice cream melts, it drips like art,
A sticky battle, a messy start.
Laughter bubbles, sweet and bright,
In this glorious glow, all feels just right.

A Tapestry of Sunlit Joy

Threads of giggles weave through the air,
Knitting smiles with the utmost care.
A funny hat, who can resist?
In this joyful chaos, I persist.

Squeaky voices, shadows collide,
Lemonade spills as I try to glide.
Here comes a seagull, misplaced jest,
But it's all in good fun—oh, what a fest!

The Enchantment of Day's Embrace

Oh, my shoulder's turned into toast,
And my nose is the buttered end, of course.
I'm a walking pancake, feeling so grand,
With sticky sweet syrup all over the land.

When bright globes take a dip in the sea,
I whip out my shades, so cool, look at me!
A lobster disguised as a sun-kissed queen,
With shades on my eyes, it's quite the scene.

My flip-flops are squeaking a silly tune,
As I dance with the shadows beneath the noon.
The heat makes my back act like a fry pan,
And yet here I stand, still part of the plan.

So grab your umbrellas, the shade is in style,
But I'll take my chances, just stay for a while.
For the laughter erupts like a fizzy drink,
Under bright beams, it's easier to blink.

Emblems of Warmth Under Skies

With a sunscreen coat, I feel like a star,
Yet my reflection says I've gone too far.
Is that a tan or a shade of baked pie?
I chuckle at this glow as I flutter by.

Sipping lemonade, it's a full-blown affair,
My straw's in a twist, like my messy hair.
While bees start to buzz and dance in the heat,
I offer them treats, just don't take my seat!

In flip-flops I trip on the runny hot sand,
And my jelly-like jiggle becomes quite a brand.
My beach towel flaps like a cartoonish kite,
As I roll and I tumble, oh what a sight!

With hats and ice-cream, we march in a line,
Each scoop melts quickly; how divine!
Laughter erupts as we slip and we slide,
In this warm bubble where fun can't hide.

Shadows Cradled in Radiance

Why did I challenge the heat to a duel?
Now I'm here sweating, like a big, silly fool.
My reflection's a peek at a comical sight,
With a smile on my face, I'm a warm-puffed delight.

Sunburn has painted my arms like a map,
A treasure of shades from a curious nap.
My flip-flop wardrobe is putting on shows,
With bows on my sandals and sparkly toes.

As the warmth tickles toes and gives life to dreams,
The clouds float by offering comical themes.
I'm juggling my sunglasses, drinks with a swirl,
Doing cartwheels amidst a fun-loving whirl.

So here's to the warmth on this silly parade,
Where laughter is vibrant and never will fade.
In the glow, we gather for laughter, for play,
With shadowy friends, we bumble away!

Echoes of Light Through Time

In the park, laughter flies,
Chasing shadows, oh what highs!
A gleam that tickles all around,
Like silly socks on grassy ground.

Ice cream drips from sticky hands,
As we dance on sun-kissed sands.
With every giggle, joy ignites,
We're time travelers, oh what sights!

Heatwaves of Memory and Euphoria

Brian's hat floats like a boat,
Got lost in laughter, what a gloat!
Sizzling chats with friends so dear,
Bubbles pop, and joys appear.

Sticky fingers on a treat,
Lemonade that smells so sweet.
In that heat, we come alive,
Our crazy antics help us thrive.

Blaze of Afternoon Delights

A picnic spread with food galore,
Sandwiches stacked, we all want more.
Giggling kids, a water fight,
Sprinklers dance, oh what a sight!

The cat's confused, she darts and leaps,
While we roll in laughter, eyes in heaps.
Peanut butter in my hair,
Moments like these, beyond compare!

Dappled Shadows in Golden Fields

Chasing bugs and dodging bees,
Swinging hats like sly trapeze.
In a field with wild delight,
We twirl and wiggle in pure light.

The neighbor's dog steals our lunch,
Taking bites in a hungry crunch.
With every pounce, our giggles bloom,
As clouds tickle us from above the gloom.

Days of Light

A giant sphere in the vast expanse,
Dancing with shadows, it leads the chance.
With every ray, a story unfolds,
Of sunburned noses and laughter bold.

Picnics scattered, ants march in line,
Chasing that ball, it's a game of design.
Yet sweat drips down like a nose on a pup,
Grinning and giggling, who'll mess with that cup?

Ice cream melting, oh what a sight,
Smeared on faces, a sugary fight.
Flip-flops flying, so carefree and bright,
These days of light, full of pure delight.

Nights of Wonder

As dusk settles in, stars peek and play,
Chasing fireflies like kids at a ballet.
A luna moth's dance, oh what a thrill,
"Who turned the lights off?" we laugh, what a spill!

S'mores in the making, chocolate goes here,
"Don't burn the marshmallows!" we joke with cheer.
With shadows that mingle, we're tales yet to weave,
In nights of wonder, we dare to believe.

The Kiss of Day's Embrace

Morning bursts forth with a giggle or two,
Bouncing and stretching, sky wears fresh dew.
"Did I just fry in that light?" one might whine,
But we dance on the grass, a day so divine.

Caffeine in hand, we plot our next feat,
Making a mess as we scurry on feet.
With each little ray, we grin and engage,
In the warmth of the morn, it's a laughter-filled stage.

Basking in the Radiant Glow

Lounge chairs lined up, a sight to be seen,
Each with a tale, all of us keen.
Sipping lemonade, all tangy and sweet,
"Oops, I spilled again!"—funny little feat.

Sands of the shore, tickling our toes,
"Watch out for crabs!" as the laughter grows.
With shades on our eyes, we laugh at our glow,
Basking in warmth, the joy starts to flow.

Wrapped in Nature's Affection

Trees whisper secrets as we tread near,
Wrapped in affection, there's nothing to fear.
"Who's ready for mud?" a voice calls with glee,
Nature's embrace, come play, come see!

Climbing up hills, it's a race to the top,
"Last one there's a rotten old mop!"
With giggles and grins under branches so grand,
We frolic through fields, all hand in hand.

Woven Warmth of the Universe

In the sky, a glowing ball,
Like nature's giant, jovial call.
Tickles on noses, smooth as cream,
A dance of rays in a silly dream.

Is that a laugh or a friendly tease?
On our cheeks, it brings us to our knees.
Dancing shadows, a quirky spree,
Melting worries, setting them free.

Threads of Light in the Evening Glow

As the day strolls into the night,
The warm threads weave a silly sight.
Giggle at shadows wearing hats,
Making faces, like silly cats.

A wink from the horizon, warm and bright,
Silly whispers dancing in flight.
Evening chuckles, a soft embrace,
The world wrapped in a glowing lace.

Illuminated by Nature's Heartbeat

Nature grins with a golden flick,
A playful pat, a gentle trick.
Like a cheeky child, frolicsome cheer,
It bounces boldly, year after year.

Under the canopy, laughter flows,
Where warmth and whimsy brightly glows.
Nature's heartbeat, a jest to share,
Each pulse a giggle in the open air.

Warmth that Wakes the Senses

A tickle here, a poke right there,
Warmth that makes you stop and stare.
It nudges you with a glow so bright,
Chasing shadows into the night.

A cheeky grin from high above,
In every beam, there's a hint of love.
So let's laugh and play, with no regret,
For warmth like this we won't forget.

Joyful Sparks of Day's Delight

A burst of giggles, bright and clear,
Chasing away the night's last fear.
Like butter melting on toast's warm fare,
Laughter dances in the glowing air.

Tickling toes as they dip in sand,
Where every grain says 'isn't life grand?'
Chasing shadows on a breezy spree,
Oh, how delightful, just you and me!

Threading Light Through the Heart

A ticklish ray peeks through the trees,
Whispering secrets with a playful tease.
Like a cat wearing a sunny hat,
It warms the chilly world like a diplomat.

Jubilant beams twirl around the day,
Painting bright colors in a child's play.
With each giggle, the moments grow bright,
As shadows retreat, dancing in delight.

A Warm Embrace from Above

A giggle from the sky, oh so grand,
Wrapping up everyone in its band.
Like cookies fresh out of a perfect bake,
It sends us all running for goodness' sake!

Fluttering high, it sprinkles some cheer,
As we chase our worries, never fear.
With every warmth, a silly dance breaks,
Sunshine and laughter — how our hearts ache!

Warmth in Every Breath

A tickle in the air, soft and light,
Wraps us around like a cozy night.
With every breath, a chuckle does bloom,
Filling our hearts, chasing away gloom.

Warm whispers giggle in our ears,
Juggling with joy, like childhood cheers.
From pinky toes to the tip of our hair,
We bask in the glow, light as a prayer.

A Dance of Light and Shadow

A beam of joy, it tickles toes,
As squirrels leap and laughter flows.
A friendly glow, it makes us grin,
While shadows play, let the frolic begin.

In a game of hide and seek so bright,
The cheeky rays are quite the sight.
They sneak around, then pounce with glee,
In this arena, we all feel free.

A hop, a skip, we glide and sway,
With every squint, we shout hooray!
For in this warmth, we feel so spry,
Dancing with shadows that flit and fly.

So come and twirl, let worries fade,
In the shimmery joy of light's parade.
With giggles loud and spirits high,
We'll laugh and leap till the day slips by.

Sunlit Whispers of the Day

Underneath those golden rays,
A whisper tickles, in playful ways.
Tickle fights with sunlight beams,
It giggles loud and stirs our dreams.

With every gleam, a joke unfolds,
Bright little secrets that light up our souls.
Elusive beams that tease our hair,
In radiant twirls, we float on air.

Grinning at clouds that drift on by,
Making faces, oh my, oh my!
In pools of light, we splash and dive,
Feeling alive—oh, how we thrive!

So let's embrace this shining spree,
As laughter dances so wild and free.
With every chuckle, we shine bright,
Celebrating day with pure delight.

Radiance that Paints the Soul

A canvas bright of giggles and glee,
As colors twirl, oh look at me!
With strokes of cheer, we brush and blend,
Creating smiles that never end.

In this playful splash of golden hue,
Sketches of laughter all around us two.
Each ray a wink, a playful lift,
In this masterpiece, we're the gift.

We paint our woes with shades so light,
Doodling dreams till they take flight.
With brush in hand and joy to seek,
We doodle sunshine, cheek to cheek.

So swirls of daylight, bright and bold,
Shimmering tales of warmth to unfold.
Brush up your giggles, let them flow,
For this radiant art we all know.

Beneath the Blazing Orb

Oh look, it's that fiery sphere,
With a sizzle, and a grin, oh dear!
It winks and nudges with a gentle burn,
And we respond with a playful turn.

Picnics under its watchful gaze,
As ants dance round in a tiny craze.
A game of hide, we scurry and leap,
Beneath the glow, my secrets keep.

With shades in hand, we wear them proud,
As laughter echoes, music loud.
The heat may rise, but so does cheer,
In this sunny carnival, we have no fear.

So let's partake in this sunny show,
With shadows laughing, putting on a glow.
Together we bask, let whimsy reign,
For under this orb, we feel no pain.

Glimmers of Hope under the Sky

In the park we run and flee,
Chasing shadows, feeling free.
Sweat beads glisten on my brow,
As I trip and take a bow.

Picnic spread upon the grass,
I munch, the ants begin to pass.
Lemonade splashes all around,
What a mess my cup has found!

Sunglasses perched upon my head,
I launch a frisbee—uh-oh, my spread!
It soars high, but what a shame,
It lands right in a pudding game!

Giggling kids glide past my sight,
All in mischief, such delight.
Under laughter, warmth and glare,
Life's a comedy, quite rare!

The Soft Glow of Afternoon

Baking cookies, what a treat,
Oven's warmth, my little seat.
But wait, what's this—a burnt delight?
Guess they're now a crunchy sight!

Ice cream drips upon my toes,
A sticky path that surely shows.
I attempt to lick it quick,
But it's gone, a magic trick!

Sipping soda, fizz flies high,
Daring friends, oh me, oh my!
With a burp that echoes wide,
I laugh at how I tried to hide.

Underneath the glowing light,
Frogs croak back, a funny sight.
Nature's jokes, they come and tease,
Even bugs want to share some cheese!

Daydreams Woven in Light

Lying down in fragrant fields,
Butterflies dance, the beauty yields.
Staring up, I dream of cakes,
But wait—what's that? A bumble's wake!

Caught in thoughts of soda fizz,
A grass stain? Oh, what a whizz!
Hiding from my mom's stern face,
As bees buzz near—please, give me space!

Giggles rise with every sunbeam,
A slip-and-slide—wow, this is a dream!
I stumble down, arms flail and spin,
Splattered mud—where do I begin?

But in these moments, joy does swell,
Taking flights where laughter dwells.
Life's a canvas, splendid, bright,
In every giggle, pure delight!

Nature's Gentle Embrace

Frolicking in meadow green,
Wobbly knee, I'm yet unseen.
Squirrel dashes 'cross my path,
I laugh and break into a laugh!

Clouds above play peek-a-boo,
A game of hide, just me and you.
Tickling leaves in the gentle breeze,
Joining in with nature's tease.

In my hat, a feathered friend,
Bouncing high, will it descend?
It lands right on my mom's fine hair,
Now they're both a sight—what a pair!

Dance of shadows, chopsticks sway,
Mimicking trees, oh what a play!
In every twist and fun parade,
Nature laughs, never afraid!

Photosynthesis of Feelings

Chasing rays like a squirrel on speed,
My skin's a canvas, nature's stampede.
Melting ice cream runs down my hand,
Best flavor? Sunshine, unplanned!

Frying eggs on the sidewalk, quite bold,
My thoughts are scrambled, but I'm not cold.
Laughter bubbles as sweat beads roll,
Who knew warmth could be so droll?

Toasting toes on the pavement's heat,
Each step's a dance, my shoes are fleet.
Flipping burgers while I twirl a straw,
Reality check: I forgot my bra!

Roasting marshmallows—oh wait, that's me!
Sweet and gooey, it's all carefree.
With every giggle, warmth I embrace,
Sunshine and laughter, life's silly chase.

Glorious Heat in an Infinite Sky

Hotter than a jalapeño's kiss,
With every ray, I find my bliss.
Sizzling smiles on a golden face,
Who needs shade? I'll dance in this space!

My flip-flops squeak more than a rat,
They plot my demise, the squeaky brat!
Snapping pics like the sun's a friend,
But my glasses kept falling, that's the trend!

Diving into puddles that should be gone,
My laughter echoes, a brightened dawn.
Each sunbeam flirts, so warm and bright,
Who knew radiance could ignite such delight?

I prance and twirl in a beachy daze,
The heat's a furnace—what a funny phase!
As freckles emerge, they start to play,
I guess my skin wanted a bright bouquet!

Sunlit Paths of Sweet Wanderings

Rambling down this sandy lane,
Each step's a giggle, none are mundane.
Friends and giggles at every turn,
A toast to warmth—may we never learn!

My hat's a circus, flopped on my brow,
A juggling act, who knew how?
Slippery ice cream, melting fast,
Life's little messes, oh what a blast!

Chasing shadows, playing tag with glee,
Blinded by joy—won't you laugh with me?
Kites in the air, dancing so bright,
I trip on my laces, what a sight!

With every misstep, we just ignite,
A symphony of giggles, pure delight.
Basking in moments, lighthearted and free,
Who needs competition, when fun's the key?

The Gold of Quiet Reflections

In this warm puddle, I see my face,
Golden rays whisper, what a place!
Each cringe from the heat, a little jolt,
Yet my happiness drips, a joyful revolt.

I'm a golden pancake, crisp but soft,
Laughing at reflections—oh, how we scoff!
Chasing dreams while sunbeams play,
Everything's funny on such a bright day!

With iced drinks clinking, we share a toast,
To the warmth that we love the most.
Melting concerns like butter on bread,
I laugh at my thoughts, totally misled!

So here's to the glow, the twinkling bright,
We'll bask in this joy, our hearts take flight.
As the day fades, let laughter remain,
In the golden reflections, we'll dance in vain.

Light's Caress through the Breeze

Oh, how it tickles, this radiant heat,
Makes my sunscreen dance and my feet feel sweet.
As I prance like a penguin on melting ice,
It feels like a party, oh isn't it nice?

With my hat askew and my shades on tight,
I wave to the clouds, oh what a sight!
I'm roasting like toast, a little too brown,
I laugh at my reflection, a sunburnt clown.

The birds are all chirping, the sky's a bright blue,
I trip on my flip-flops, say 'Who even knew?'
Yet here in this dazzle, my heart skips and sings,
In the warmth of this laughter, oh what joy spring brings!

So come join the fun, let's dance in the rays,
We'll pretend we're in movies, in silly sun plays.
With everyone giggling, it's a sight to behold,
In this golden embrace, we'll never grow old!

Illuminated Moments of Joy

Under this glow, I'm a happy little bug,
With cheeks like ripe cherries and an extra hug.
The heat's got me laughing, I can't take it slow,
Trying to find shade but the sun says 'No!'

I drop my ice cream, oh what a big mess,
It splats on the sidewalk, it's anyone's guess.
The kids all giggle, they point and they shriek,
As I make a quick dash for the shade like a freak.

With lemonade splashes and bright t-shirt stains,
Each moment of warmth cures all of my pains.
To jump in the pool and forget all my cares,
Just pass me the floaties, my laughs fill the air!

The day seems to sparkle, each grin is so wide,
I'm caught in the riddle of summer's big tide.
With friends all around, let's bask in this light,
These illuminated moments feel just so right!

The Brightness of Being Alive

In this cheerful haze, my worries take flight,
With laughter like bubbles that float in pure light.
I trip on my sandals, do a silly dance,
Each sunbeam a wink, each moment a chance.

The world seems to shimmer, oh what a delight,
I squint at the sky, it's too bright for my sight.
A squirrel steals my chips, and the laughter erupts,
As I scratch my own head, like a goose that's been cupped.

With popsicles dripping, I wear all the colors,
Each flavor an explosion, like candy for brothers.
We run through the fields, chasing nothing but air,
In this brightness of living, we've got naught a care.

So let's toast to today with our fizzy drinks high,
With sunburned noses and a sparkling sky.
Together we giggle, in this radiance thrive,
Embracing the joy that's the brightness of being alive!

Embracing Celestial Warmth

In this celestial hug, I'm a star on the ground,
With sweat on my brow, I twirl round and round.
Each ray like a giggle, a wink from the sky,
It pulls me like gravity, oh my, oh my!

I wear flip-flops loud, like a marching parade,
And every step makes me feel like I've made
A fashion statement, oh so avant-garde,
I strut in my towel, like I'm fresh from the yard.

With friends all beside me, we share all the feels,
Ice cream as treasure, oh what a big deal!
A sprinkle tornado, a cone falls and thrills,
As we race down the street, all laughter and spills.

So here's to the moments, the warmth and the glow,
In robes of pure laughter, we'll steal every show.
When the day turns to night, and we sit and reflect,
We'll cherish the warmth that we couldn't neglect!

Silhouettes Beneath the Horizon

In the heat, we dance with glee,
Our shadows leap, wild and free.
Sunglasses perched, a fashion scene,
Like movie stars, we strut and preen.

Ice cream drips down on our toes,
Sticky joy that everyone knows.
We laugh as a seagull swoops low,
Stealing bites from our sunlit show.

Flip-flops flapping, what a sound,
As we chase ballads, round and round.
With beach towels laid like canvases,
We paint our lives with goofy grins.

The horizon smiles with a golden wink,
While we tumble, trip, and overthink.
But oh, the laughter that we share,
Under the blaring light, we dare.

Sunlit Whispers in the Air

In the park, the rays do tease,
With lemonade and a gentle breeze.
We fan ourselves, make a fuss,
It's too hot, but who cares? Let's discuss!

A squirrel steals our snacks with flair,
Chasing it down, we leap with dare.
Our hair a mess, sunscreen spread,
Like pasta sauce, we laugh instead.

Picnic ants march on parade,
In the shade, our worries fade.
Selfie sticks at awkward angles,
Captured smiles with silly tangles.

As loopy as a summer's day,
We tumble in giggles, come what may.
With every splash in the nearby brook,
We write our story without a book.

Caress of Celestial Fire

We swelter under a flaming grin,
While tiny sweat beads race our chin.
Hats too big, we trip and fall,
Our antics echo, a discordant call.

The barbecue sizzles, smoke rings soar,
Each flip of the burger—what a chore!
With ketchup battles we wage in fun,
Messy faces under the run.

Beachballs fly like comets bright,
Dodging them, we clutch and fight.
The laughter roars as kids all squeal,
Drenched in joy, it feels surreal.

The evening wanes, our cheeks all bright,
With stories told under starry light.
We hold our sides from laughing so,
Under that blaze, our spirits glow.

Fragments of Morning Glow

Wake up early, chase the rays,
Breakfast dance in quirky ways.
Cereal spills, a cheerful mess,
A breakfast bowl, now a dress!

With sandals mismatched, we step outside,
A stroll with friends, a sunny ride.
We wave at clouds, attempt a jog,
But soon it's back to our lazy slog.

The birds sing tunes, we sing along,
In harmony, we still get it wrong.
Our off-key notes cause giggles wide,
As we embrace the sunny tide.

Lazy days turn to wild night,
With fireflies twinkling, what a sight!
As stars peek through the twilight's curtain,
The laughter echoes, oh, it's certain!

When Light Meets the Body

I tried to tan, oh what a plight,
My bathing suit's a shocking sight.
Spots that gleam in varying shades,
Who knew my skin could play charades?

A flip-flop tan, so bold, so fine,
My feet are white, my legs divine.
With lotion slick, I dance and prance,
A comedy show, not a romance!

I thought I'd glow, a golden hue,
But ended up with lobster stew.
Friends chuckle, point, and take a snap,
I claim my tan is just a chap!

In the bright rays, I slip and slide,
Chasing shadows, nowhere to hide.
Next year I vow to plan ahead,
And wear a hat that's big and red!

Serenade of Sunlit Dreams

With rays that dance on my warm face,
I wander freely, full of grace.
My joy spills out like melting ice,
Avoiding squirrels, oh, what a price!

With each bright beam, a comical scene,
I trip and tumble while feeling keen.
A bird swoops low, I scream and shout,
"Hey, feathered friend! You've got clout!"

Picnic spreads with food galore,
But ants parade, they want some more.
I laugh as they invade my feast,
"Fine, my friends, you're quite the beast!"

As shadows stretch and laughter grows,
I break into a funny pose.
For sunlit dreams are here to stay,
At least 'til I'm too tired to play!

Transience of a Day's Gilded Hues

A morning stretch, I bask in light,
The struggle's real, a glorious fight.
I sip my coffee, the warmth sedates,
But get distracted—oh, look! A bait!

With cheerful birds, I start to hum,
Yet sunburn sneaks in, it's quite the bum.
I laugh and lather, a lotion spree,
Though it seems more like a slippery plea!

As clouds parade with shadows thick,
I dodge their trick like a playful flick.
In my sunhat, I look absurd,
But this kind of funny? It's preferred!

So here I stand, with colors bold,
A polka-dot suit, I'm sun-kissed gold.
Each fleeting ray brings laughs anew,
In gilded hues, life feels like a zoo!

Solstice Dreams on Bare Shoulders

I strut outside, a summer queen,
With bare shoulders, oh so keen.
The rays applaud, a bright encore,
While I dodge bees, and scream for more!

A beach ball bounces with silly flair,
I miss the catch—just lots of air!
My friends all fall, a comedic mess,
But hey, that's life, a sunny jest!

A barbecue sizzles, laughter spills,
I'm the chef, with dubious skills.
Charred sausages? Oh, what a feat,
Next year, I swear, I'll watch the heat!

With sun-soaked nights and stories grand,
We sip cool drinks from mismatched cans.
The warmth of friendship, laughter rings,
In solstice dreams, we find our flings!

Embracing the Warmth of Daylight

A chicken in shades, struts with flair,
It dances around to the warm, bright air.
Fried eggs wave hello from the pan,
Sizzling laughter from a sunny clan.

The ice cream melts, drips down my hand,
I chase after it, isn't it grand?
Life's too short for a frown or a sigh,
Bring on the joy and let's jump high!

Touch of Radiance

My buddy splashed sunscreen with glee,
But missed his nose, oh what a sight to see!
Now his face is a lighthouse, shining so bright,
He's a beacon of laughter from morning to night.

We played frisbee, a glorious game,
But hit a seagull, oh what a shame!
The bird squawked loud in its skyward flight,
As our giggles echoed, a comical plight.

Sun-Kissed Dreams Unfold

The sand between toes and a drink in hand,
A squirrel appears, bold, unplanned.
He grabs my sandwich, what a cheeky bite,
While I just sit back, basking in delight.

A splash of water, oh what a blunder,
I fell in the pool, but now I'm a thunder!
Chasing my friends, it's a playful race,
With giggles and splashes, we conquer the place.

Solar Serenade on Bare Shoulders

An ice-cold drink, but my straw's gone rogue,
It tickles my nose, oh what a fogue!
The laughter that bounces, a joy so loud,
We're a merry little band, oh aren't we proud?

A butterfly lands on my silly hat,
It's dressed up in style—what's next, a cat?
We cheer for our friends who brave a bright jump,
Splashing in puddles with a joyful thump.

Radiant Echoes of Childhood

In the park, we run and play,
Chasing shadows, night turns to day.
Ice cream drips on little toes,
Laughter spills like a garden hose.

Sticky fingers, grass-stained knees,
Hiding from the summer breeze.
Silly songs are sung out loud,
Parents roll their eyes, so proud.

Tiny hands paint on the wall,
Magical moments, we recall.
With every splash and joyful cheer,
Childhood dreams feel so near.

Days like this, who needs a plan?
A cardboard box turns to a van.
Giggles echo through the air,
Who knew life could be so rare?

Twilight's Farewell to Daylight

The sky blushes, hues combined,
As bedtime stories interwind.
Pajamas on, we race for crumbs,
Sneaking snacks, oh, here it comes!

Socks mismatched, a daring feat,
Bouncing on a trampoline seat.
With wobbly legs, we dance around,
Pretending we're the sky unbound.

Outfit's a mess and hair's a fright,
Chaos reigns until goodnight.
Whispers fill the late-night air,
With giggles, we create our lair.

Toothpaste battles each time we brush,
Bedtime socks, oh what a fuss!
Twilight laughs as we conclude,
In dreams, we're all in a happy mood!

Breaths of Warmth in Quiet Corners

A blanket fort, our secret dome,
Where made-up worlds become our home.
Flashlight beams dance on the walls,
In hidden paths where magic calls.

Nibbles tucked in every nook,
Creature comforts, there's no book.
We giggle softly, sharing a breath,
Inventing tales that spark new quests.

Sunshine streams through the curtains wide,
As pillow fights become our pride.
In the quiet, we plant our dreams,
In victory dances, nothing's as it seems.

Whispers weave through evening light,
In our fortress, everything's right.
With every breath, a breeze of joy,
Every corner holds a brand new ploy!

Shimmering Mosaic of Joy

Rainbows sprout on rainy days,
Splashing puddles in a wild craze.
Dancing ducks in wobbly lines,
Silly hats and mismatched designs.

A woozy waddle, a feathery chase,
Squirrels scamper, oh what a race!
Crayon colors burst and bloom,
Painting joy, we'll light the room.

With every giggle, the world awakes,
Ice cream dreams, oh, what a cake!
Jumping high on swings that tease,
Time slips away with perfect ease.

We'll build a castle made of cheer,
With every laugh, we'll conquer fear.
In the shimmer of our playful dance,
Life's a tapestry of sweet romance!

Sunshine Echoing Through Time

A golden orb doth dance and sway,
Melting all the clouds away.
With rays that tickle, tease, and poke,
It's summer's laugh, a laughter's joke.

The shadows stretch, they twist and bend,
As if the day has time to spend.
Invisible hands play hide and seek,
In this warm glow, I'm far from meek.

Oh, how it radiates a cheerful beam,
Like a chocolate kiss, or whipped cream dream.
I chase my hat that flies like a kite,
And giggle at birds in mid-flight.

So here I sit in blissful glee,
With rays that shout, "Come, play with me!"
In this golden soup, I stew, I fry,
And wave at clouds that drift on by.

A Symphony of Warmth and Light

A bright parade of light so spry,
Bumbles 'round, oh my, oh my!
It drizzles warmth like melted cheese,
I catch the drops with such great ease.

A tickle here, a shimmer there,
It flips my hair without a care.
Each beam a note in nature's tune,
A waltz with clouds, a dance with noon.

The squirrels join in a sunny jig,
While flowers bloom, and don't dig!
They stretch their petals to say, "Why not?"
In this warm concert, we all trot.

So take a bow, you cheeky rays,
Your brilliance brightens all my days.
In this grand hall of laughter and light,
I twirl and whirl, oh, what a sight!

Twirl of Light in Open Fields

In fields of gold, I skip and roll,
As bright beams tickle at my soul.
With every twist, I laugh with glee,
A dandelion's dance, just like me!

The breezes whisper jokes so coy,
They rattle 'round in purest joy.
The glow, it winks, it hugs my face,
In this warm circus, I find my place.

Grass stains sneak into my best clothes,
A little mischief that nobody knows.
I chase my shadow, oh so spry,
My feet a flurry, reaching for the sky.

So come, dear friends, let's twirl along,
With beams of laughter, silly and strong.
In these open fields, let's bask and play,
Under this cheer, hip-hip-hooray!

Morning Glories Underneath the Light

Morning blooms with giggles loud,
Waking up the sleepy crowd.
Petals stretch with a sunny grin,
As daylight whispers, "Let's begin!"

With swirls of color, they make a trumpet,
Loud enough that you can't just plump it.
The grass beneath, a plush delight,
Laughs quietly in the morning light.

I stumble through with messy hair,
While bees take turns doing their share.
A minor tug, a juicy drop,
As laughter bounces, I just can't stop.

So here's to mornings, cheerful and bright,
With glorious smiles, in daring flight.
In a world so warm, I gleefully dwell,
Thanking the morning for all it compels!

Harmony Found in Solar Touch

Golden beams play tag with sight,
While I try to find my right.
A dance of warmth upon my face,
Making melting ice cream chase.

I search for shade, but oh so bright,
It tickles me, a pure delight.
My friends all laugh, they see me grin,
As sweat drips like a chilly sin.

Frog legs jiggling, shorts and tanks,
A bronzed parade, with plenty pranks.
Each laugh a ray, each joke a beam,
Feeling silly, in a sun-kissed dream.

The beach, a blast, with sand as gold,
Playing catch with sun, so bold.
Life's a joke when warmth prevails,
In the glow, no one fails.

Flickering Flames of Day's Heart

Mornings bright, I squint and squawk,
Coffee spills as I try to walk.
I chase my hat, oh what a sight,
It flies away in pure delight.

Sizzling sidewalks, scalding toes,
Running fast, where laughter grows.
A sunburn patch that looks quite rare,
Now I'm an art piece, full of flair.

Picnic plans that go askew,
Ants arriving, oh what a crew!
We munch on sandwiches and cheese,
While dodging bites from buzzing bees.

The sunset drips, a paintbrush bold,
Tickling noses, casting gold.
Life's a sketch, a lively jest,
With flickering flames, we're all so blessed.

Golden Rays of Embrace

Laughter echoes on the shore,
Each golden ray, I want more.
That playful poke from the light,
Stirs up a dance, oh what a sight.

Umbrellas flop and sunglasses fly,
Tanned toes peek, say hi, oh my!
A clumsy slip, a leap, a fall,
I bounce right back; I'll take it all.

Grilled delights turn BBQ fun,
We're sizzling up 'til day is done.
I spill my drink, it's all a game,
With laughter loud, who feels the shame?

When evening glows, we gather round,
Stories shared with joy profound.
Under stars, we revel and cheer,
Golden moments, forever near.

Warmth in a Summer's Gaze

Oh the rays that tease and pleat,
Make my ice cream melt, so sweet.
A dance of clumsy happy feet,
While grass stains make the day complete.

Hats are flying, kids go wild,
And we all stand, so sun-begiled.
My friend's got shade, and I just laugh,
As I steal it back, in my own path.

Water fights become our wars,
I'm drenched and squishy, to the core.
Beach balls bouncing like they're free,
Sunkissed life, full of glee.

When twilight wraps, we share our hearts,
A golden glow, that never departs.
Framed in warmth, we hold our place,
In memories bright, we find our grace.

In the Light's Gentle Grasp

Warmth on my shoulders, a hug from above,
As I dance like a chicken, forgetting my love.
Sweat on my brow, it's a glistening sheen,
Oh, how I twirl in this pale golden sheen!

The laughter around me, it tickles my toes,
With each playful step, my confidence grows.
Tanning my awkwardness beneath glowing rays,
I'm a hot mess of charm on these dazzling days!

Friends tease me gently, 'Are you melting away?'
I roll my eyes back, 'Let's frolic and play!'
With sunscreen a must, we lather and glide,
Call me a butter, I'm slipping with pride!

So here's to the gleam that brightens my grin,
And to every wild moment that bubbles within.
I'll wear this warm glow like a quirky old friend,
In the light's gentle grasp, let the fun never end!

The Light that Awakens Dreams

Awake with a giggle, all dreams in a whirl,
I stumble outdoors, I'm a spinning top girl.
Bright beams pull me out like a spoon from a bowl,
It's breakfast with laughter, my ultimate goal!

Skipping through puddles, I'm soaking in cheer,
With each little splash, I forget all my fear.
Sandals are stuck, in the muck I reside,
But it's fine, I'm just dancing, my bubbly pride!

The clouds are conspiring, they're tickling my fate,
As I breathe in the warmth, isn't laughter great?
I'm sun-kissed and silly, with mischief in tow,
Each ray is a nudge to just let my heart glow!

So here's to the spark that awakens my muse,
With each shining moment, I've got nothing to lose.
Chasing bright daydreams as they swirl and gleam,
In a world full of giggles, I'll dance and I'll beam!

Echoes of Heat and Harmony

The air's like a blanket, a hug that won't quit,
Roasting my neurons, I giggle and sit.
With friends in a circle, I bask in the jest,
Life is a circus, and I'm just a guest!

Hot dogs are grilling with playful delight,
I sing to the rhythm, a hot-headed sprite.
A fly buzzes past, I swat with finesse,
But it dodges my hand—what a sly little pest!

Melodies float, as we sway in the blaze,
Ice cream in hand, wearing sticky buffays.
We laugh at our blunders—who wears it with pride?
In this heat of the moment, I twirl and I glide!

So raise up your glass, let's toast to the fun,
Each giggle and snort, let's cherish each one.
In echoes of heat, where humor aligns,
I'll sway with the rhythm, till the silver sun declines!

Brightness Between Heartbeats

Bouncing on sidewalks with joy in my stride,
I'm caught in the glow, and there's nowhere to hide.
The world's like a stage, I'm the star of the show,
With freckles and laughter, I'm ready to go!

Faces turn bright and it's clear that I shine,
Witty comebacks flow, they're simply divine.
A dog chases shadows, it jumps and it spins,
Meanwhile, I'm here rocking my sun-kissed chins!

Waving to strangers, as I zigzag and whirl,
Making friends in the warmth—watch my laughter unfurl.

Why bother with worries when life's full of quirk?
In the light's playful blink, I'm ready to perk!

The brightness is here, dancing right in my chest,
In the heartbeat of laughter, I'll simply invest.
So let whimsy prevail on this shimmering ride,
For happiness lingers, like the joy I cannot hide!

Golden Embrace of Daylight

A golden glow upon my back,
I cherish it like a good snack.
It tickles me, oh what a treat,
Making my sunburns feel so neat.

With shades of laughter, I do prance,
In this radiant, yellow dance.
I pose like a sizzling fry,
With heat that makes the locusts sigh.

The world is bright; my skin's on fire,
I'm a toasted human, oh so dire!
But I can't help but grin and bask,
In this burning hug, I'm up to the task.

So here I go, enjoying the rays,
While my laughter echoes like sun-filled days.
I'll take my chances, roll the dice,
To glow and giggle, oh how nice!

Warmth That Kisses the Surface

It whispers sweetly on my cheek,
A cheeky warmth, so mild, yet sleek.
A playful hug from the high above,
Making this moment feel like love.

I stroll around, my skin aglow,
People squint; just look at me go!
Like a muffin fresh out of the pan,
Oh, how egg-cited is this tan!

Belly laughs mix with the heat,
While jolly rhythms bounce on my feet.
I become a walking toasted loaf,
In this sunlight, I'm at my most dope!

So bring on the giggles, let's have some fun,
As sunbeams tickle, I'm overrun!
With every glimmer, my joy's unchained,
In this warm embrace, I'm thoroughly entertained!

Radiance Dancing on Flesh

There's a jiggle, a wiggle, on my arm,
A radiant dance, oh such a charm!
Laughter erupts with every ray,
As I try to find my playful sway.

It's questionable how I didn't explode,
With hues of orange, I corrode.
I'm the comical crispy thing,
In my own parade, let the giggles ring!

Oh, how the breeze teases my hair,
Making me feel like a fairground flare.
As I twist and turn with all my might,
Becoming a jelly that's lost the fight!

So let's spin to this golden beat,
With each twirl, I'm feeling upbeat!
In the spectacle of wild displays,
I'll be the star of the sunny rays!

Laughter of the Warm Breeze

A warm wind tickles the tips of my toes,
Whispers of giggles where nobody knows.
On the edge of mirth, I bounce and sway,
Like a leaf on a journey, I'm eager to play.

It lifts me high, in a playful tease,
Turning strong into gentle, like a warm breeze.
My cheeks go rosy, all plump and round,
In this jocular warmth, oh what a sound!

I drift like a balloon, so silly and free,
With winds that sing songs just for me.
Every chuckle rises, a joyful song,
In a madcap dance, where I truly belong!

So come, let us frolic, let's skip and glide,
In this realm of laughter, there's nothing to hide.
With each gust of mirth, I'm filled with delight,
In this funny frolic, everything feels right!

www.ingramcontent.com/pod-product-compliance
Lightning Source LLC
Chambersburg PA
CBHW072121070526
44585CB00016B/1523